TRADITIONS AND CELEBRATIONS

MARDI GRAS

by Laura K. Murray

PEBBLE
a capstone imprint

Published by Pebble, an imprint of Capstone
1710 Roe Crest Drive, North Mankato, Minnesota 56003
capstonepub.com

Library of Congress Cataloging-in-Publication Data is available on the Library of Congress website.
ISBN: 9798875284373 (hardcover)
ISBN: 9798875284328 (paperback)
ISBN: 9798875284335 (ebook PDF)

Summary: Readers will discover the history of Mardi Gras and the many ways people around the world celebrate it.

Editorial Credits
Editor: Carrie Sheely; Designer: Heidi Thompson; Media Researcher: Rebekah Hubstenberger; Production Specialist: Tori Abraham

Image Credits
Getty Images: ampueroleonardo, 29, Awakening, 24, Buda Mendes, 1, Carl Court, 20, Chip Somodevilla, 7, Hulton Archive, 9, Jonathan Bachman, 18, Michael DeMocker, 15, 16, Peter Macdiarmid, 6, powerofforever, 10, Sean Gardner, 14, Skip Bolen, 17, Spencer Platt, 13, Wagner Meier, 23; Library of Congress: Prints & Photographs Division, 11; Newscom: BILL GREENBLATT/UPI, 19; Shutterstock: A.PAES, 22, Andreas Mann, 27, FooTToo, 25, Jennifer White Maxwell, cover, Kobby Dagan, 26, Rawpixel.com, 8, Roberto Galan, 28, vetre, 21, William A. Morgan, 5, 12

Design Elements
Shutterstock: Rafal Kulik

Printed and bound in China. 006459

TABLE OF CONTENTS

Words in **bold** are in the glossary.

What Is Mardi Gras?

Let the party begin! Music fills the air. People line the streets and watch the colorful parade floats go past. Dancers spin in bright costumes. At night, fireworks light up the sky.

Mardi Gras (*MAR*-dee *grah*) means “Fat Tuesday” in French. It is a celebration before the **Christian** season of **Lent** begins. Mardi Gras takes place in February or March.

Catholics attend Mass on Ash Wednesday.

Mardi Gras is the day before Ash Wednesday. For Christians, Ash Wednesday marks the start of Lent. Lent lasts 40 days before Easter. For many Christians, Lent is a serious time. People pray. They may **fast**. Some people give up treats such as chocolate or coffee.

On Ash Wednesday, pastors mark people's foreheads with ashes.

Mardi Gras has roots in history and **religion**. In ancient Rome, people gathered before spring came. They prayed to the Roman gods. They held festivals that included food and dancing.

An ancient Roman festival

A newspaper illustration shows a Mardi Gras celebration in Genoa, Italy, in the late 1800s.

Later, the **Catholic** religion spread through Europe. People celebrated before Lent. Old **traditions** mixed with new religious beliefs. People moved to other parts of the world. They brought their traditions with them.

Mardi Gras History

The French brought Mardi Gras to the United States. In March 1699, explorers camped along the Mississippi River in present-day Louisiana. It was the day before Mardi Gras. They then named the area after the holiday.

In 1703, people celebrated the first Mardi Gras in the United States. It was in Mobile, Alabama.

Explorer Pierre Le Moyne d'Iberville named the spot near the Mississippi River. He called it Pointe du Mardi Gras.

A Mardi Gras celebration in New Orleans in the early 1900s

By the 1800s, celebrations had grown. In 1857, the first Mardi Gras parade was held in New Orleans. Today, thousands of people visit the city of New Orleans for Mardi Gras.

Sometimes, the celebrations leading up to Mardi Gras are called Carnival. They may last days or weeks. Mardi Gras is Carnival's last day.

In Christianity, January 6 is called the Twelfth Night. The date marks the end of the Christmas season. The Twelfth Night also kicks off Carnival in New Orleans.

A Mardi Gras parade in New Orleans

A Mardi Gras celebration in Port-au-Prince, Haiti

Time to Celebrate

Mardi Gras and Carnival parades have music, singing, and dancing. People wear feathers and beads. Some dress as fairies or clowns. In New Orleans, people crown the King of Carnival. The king's parade is the Rex Parade.

The King of Carnival in the Rex Parade

Mardi Gras colors are bright purple, green, and gold. Purple stands for justice. Green stands for faith. Gold means power. The colors likely came from the Rex Parade in 1892.

People on floats toss items to the parade crowds. The items are called "throws." People try to catch beads, coins, stuffed animals, and small prizes.

In New Orleans, some parades take place at night. A group of people carry flaming torches. The torches light the parade route. Dancing and torch twirling entertains the crowds. In the past, people carried heavy wooden torches. Today, the torches are much lighter and safer to carry.

People dance at Mardi Gras balls. They dress up in fancy clothes. New Orleans has groups called krewes. They plan the balls, parades, and other events. The city has more than 100 balls each year.

Masks are a big part of Mardi Gras tradition. Years ago, people of the lower **class** could not speak to people of the higher class. But masks hid who everyone was. People could celebrate together.

People in Mardi Gras costumes at a ball in St. Louis

Mardi Gras is sometimes called Pancake Tuesday. Many people follow religious rules during Lent. They give up some foods. Hundreds of years ago, people gave up eggs, milk, and butter. They wanted to use up the foods before Lent. So they made pancakes! Today, people still eat pancakes on Mardi Gras.

In London, England, some people hold pancake races on Mardi Gras.

King cake

King cake is another holiday food. It has purple, gold, and green icing. Inside is a small plastic baby figure. It is a symbol for baby Jesus. The person who finds the baby is said to have good luck. It also means that person is responsible for bringing the king cake the next year.

Around the World

People celebrate Carnival and Mardi Gras around the world. The largest Carnival is in Rio de Janeiro, Brazil. It lasts about a week. More than 2 million people come to the city each day. There are parties in the streets. Parades have beautiful costumes and floats.

A musical performance during Carnival in Rio de Janeiro

Members of a samba school compete in Rio de Janeiro.

A large samba competition is held in Brazil. Samba is a lively dance and music style. The dance has fast footwork and a lot of hip movement. The competing samba schools plan their dance, music, costumes, and **theme**. Many schools use historical themes about people and past events.

The Flight of the Angel in Venice, Italy

Venice, Italy, is famous for its Carnival masks. The masks may look like animals or characters. People row boats in a night parade on water. In the town square, a woman dresses as an angel. She flies over the crowd attached to a cable.

In Germany, there are parades, parties, and music. People wear masks made of wood. They may dress as witches, animals, and more.

A Carnival parade in Germany

Belgium's famous Carnival lasts three days. People wear wax masks. Their shoes are wooden clogs. They throw oranges to the crowd. The oranges are for good luck. Parades and fireworks add to the fun.

A Carnival parade in Binche, Belgium

A Carnival parade in Basel, Switzerland

In Basel, Switzerland, a parade begins in the early morning. City lights are turned off. People wear head lanterns to light the way. Later, there are more parades. Big groups show off their parade costumes.

Mardi Gras is a time for joy and fun. Many Mardi Gras traditions around the world are similar. But they have differences too. Mardi Gras is a good reminder of how traditions blend with new ones over time. What's your favorite Mardi Gras tradition?

CHICKEN
DAIQUIRI
T-SHIRTS
Marching Unit

GLOSSARY

Catholic (KATH-o-lik)—following the religion of the Roman Catholic Church

Christian (KRIS-chee-AN)—someone who believes in and follows the teachings of Jesus Christ

class (CLASS)—a group of people who are similar in things like wealth, work, and education

fast (FAST)—to give up food or drink for a certain amount of time, often for a religious or spiritual reason

Lent (LENT)—a time in Christian faiths, lasting the 40 days before Easter

religion (ree-LIJ-uhn)—a system of belief, faith, and worship

theme (THEEM)—a subject or topic

tradition (truh-DISH-uhn)—a custom, idea, or belief passed down through time

READ MORE

Bolte, Mari. *Christian Festivals and Traditions*. North Mankato, MN: Capstone, 2025.

Borgert-Spaniol, Megan. *Winter Crafts Across Cultures: 12 Projects to Celebrate the Season*. North Mankato, MN: Capstone, 2023.

Foran, Jill. *Mardi Gras*. New York: Smartbook Media, 2021.

INTERNET SITES

Ducksters: Mardi Gras
ducksters.com/holidays/mardi_gras.php

National Geographic Kids: Shrove Tuesday Facts
natgeokids.com/uk/discover/geography/general-geography/shrove-tuesday-facts/

PBS: Mardi Gras
thinktv.pbslearningmedia.org/resource/ba0489a6-3111-4dfe-8c1e-0ed90784aa8a/Mardi-gras-all-about-the-holidays

INDEX

ABOUT THE AUTHOR

Laura K. Murray is the Minnesota-based author of more than 100 books for young readers. She loves helping others find their own story! Visit her at LauraKMurray.com.